NOT DONE YET

MOVING FORWARD
THROUGH GRIEF

Heidi Kubin

Prominence Publishing

www.prominencepublishing.com

The author can be reached through www.heidikubin.com

Cover photography by Sharla Pike.

Not Done Yet—Moving Forward Through Grief / Heidi Kubin — 1st ed.

ISBN: 978-1-988925-79-0

This book is dedicated to all the grievers
No matter the size or the source, I see you.

Table of Contents

ACKNOWLEDGEMENTS

There have been SO MANY beautiful souls that have helped make this book happen, and I want to acknowledge every single one of you.

Getting here, to this point in my journey, would absolutely not be possible without the love and support of so many. And if you are wondering if this might be you, IT IS. A small gesture, a text message, a meal, an encouraging thought, sending me love and strength, helping through the small and big details of these last few years. It is not lost on me that I am so well loved. I am eternally and deeply grateful for this.

A few specific thank yous are in order as well…

Sarah Murphy-Kangas and Jasmine Lemon. The insights, wisdom, and time you contributed to this book were invaluable. Thank you for your honest and loving feedback.

Suzanne Doyle-Ingram and the whole team at Prominence Publishing. I am so grateful for your partnership in this project, your enthusiasm and belief in my story.

My family. The one I was born into, and the one I married into. Your endless love, support, and belief in me is foundational to who I am.

My girls, Jenna and Kendra. You are my heart and my inspiration. Being your mama is my greatest joy. You are the most beautiful expression of your dad and I, and this will always be my greatest gift. Together, we have learned strength and resilience and have a whole lot of fun doing it too. I will love you with my whole heart for all of my days.

My late husband, Travis. Loving you and being loved by you profoundly changed me. For every one of my days, I will be grateful for the opportunity to be your wife. This journey of healing has you scribbled all over it – in the adventure, strength, and vulnerability of it all. It will always be me and you, babe. It just looks a little different now.

INTRODUCTION

On October 19th, 2018, my husband dropped dead. Travis was a healthy, full-of-life 47-year-old man. Our twin daughters were 19 and just starting their second year of university. We had a lot of life and a lot of loving ahead of us.

I was out of town and got the phone call you never want to get—only to then have to make the phone calls you never want to have to make—calling our daughters to crush their worlds as well. Somehow, we got home and met a house full of people and began to absorb the shock of this life-changing loss.

The very next day, I set out before the sun rose with my daughters and a dear friend to hike up a mountain behind our house, watch the sunrise, and be together as we began to let this new reality settle in. On the way back down the mountain, just moments from the top, I stepped off a rock (apparently the wrong way) and broke my left tibia and fibula. I WAS AT THE TOP OF A MOUNTAIN! I was taken to the hospital, went into surgery, and came out with two plates and 13 screws in my leg.

Come on!!!

I have spent much of my time since then learning how to grieve. I remember at some point during the first few days after my husband died thinking, "I am going to grieve well." I don't think I really knew what that meant, and I don't know if there is such a thing as doing it right or well. But I think what I meant was, I wanted to *feel* this thing. I didn't want to numbly accept the unthinkable. I wanted to feel, struggle and learn something from it. I knew, at that early stage, that was the only way I would be able to begin to mend my heart in any kind of meaningful way.

And oh, sweet Jesus, have I felt, struggled, and learned—more than I could have ever imagined. I also know that I'm not done yet. There is more coming, I am certain. When you're struggling through an impossibly difficult situation, an overabundance of quotes and sayings seems to come your way. Most of them have the intention of providing some comfort to our broken hearts. Some have been helpful, and some have not. And please, do not get me started on the chorus that in one way or another resembles "God has a plan for you." Mmhm. Please take your God who has a plan for me and gently place it in the section that sees no sunshine. What I did find helpful was the idea that the deeper you love, the deeper you grieve, or some version of this or some version of this. For me, this was helpful. It validated the great love that belonged to my husband and I, and it prepared me for a long journey of grieving him.

I have felt and will continue to feel so much. Throughout this story, you will hear how my heart has become intimate with heartbreak, loneliness, worry, jealousy. I am familiar with feeling misunderstood, lost, afraid, invisible, and frustrated.

I have struggled. The process of grief is not a linear one. It is not exclusive to one feeling at a time. Grief is unpredictable and messy. It is full of contradictions and repetitions. Just when I think I have "gotten through" a particular aspect of grief, it comes back in some new and annoying form. I don't love this. I would like a workbook that I could go through, working on one particular aspect at a time, checking things off, and feeling confident that I have dealt with it and am ready to move on. Remember those spelling tests in elementary school when you studied your cute little overall-wearing bum off for the scratch and sniff sticker to tell you that you did it right? I want that sticker on my neatly packaged grief process. Also, make it the bubble gum scent, please. That was my favorite. Unfortunately, it doesn't work this way. I have struggled with this unpredictable journey, frustrated that I couldn't be stronger, more independent, more assured.

And I have learned. This has been the surprising beauty within this heartache. My heart has broken, and it has also expanded to include so much more: More empathy, more patience, more grace, more openness, and more gratitude.

I have also learned that grief does not solely belong to those who have had a beloved leave this earth. Grief casts a wide net. In addition to death, it can also capture those who find themselves:

- At the end of a relationship
- Battling health issues with themselves or someone they love
- Coping with unmet expectations—the reality of what they have been working on isn't as great as they hoped it would be
- Disappointed with their current situation not matching what "was supposed to be"
- At a point of financial trouble
- Losing a job
- Facing changing roles within a relationship
- Entering a new phase of life

Essentially, you can feel grief after any event that leaves you thinking, "This is not what I had planned..." or "What the actual F is happening?"

In many ways, the process of grief is similar regardless of the source. My own grief has arisen from losing my husband. However, I have noticed similar feelings with people in my life who are going through a divorce, entering retirement, facing a newly empty nest, and managing unhealthy friendships.

When your partner dies, people have pretty deep pockets of empathy, love, understanding, and patience. Do they extend these same courtesies to other sources of grief? Do we extend this to ourselves? I wonder if acknowledging that grief comes from a wider variety of sources than we usually assume would it give us permission to extend an extra dose of these to ourselves and others?

Grief is inevitable. We all experience loss. If we can name it when it shows up, perhaps we can navigate the process with more awareness and grace. Through my own process of grief, I have found several sources of comfort and healing. They have guided me and supported me in this process. Regardless of what you are grieving, my hope is that you can find comfort and courage in your process.

I need you to know that I am not an expert on grief. I do not have it figured out. And to be honest, I don't actually think figuring it out is possible. I am just living through a devastating loss. I have experienced deep grief, and I'm still here. Some days are good, and other days I can't get my shit together. I'm a human being trying to navigate my way through life and grief. Each person experiences grief in their own way; this is mine.

I do believe that telling our stories is what connects us. Part of my story may resonate with part of your story. And through this, we are connected.

MY STORY

"We're wired for story. In a culture of scarcity and perfectionism, there's a surprisingly simple reason we want to own, integrate, and share our stories of struggle. We do this because we feel the most alive when we're connecting with others and being brave with our stories—it's in our biology."
- Brene Brown, *Rising Strong*

I believe there is so much power in sharing our stories. Stories honor our own experiences and, perhaps more importantly, they connect us with others. When we share our stories, our own experiences are validated and understood. Stories also allow for different perspectives, providing a thoughtful reflection on unique experiences.

So, here's my story.

Just over two weeks after Travis died, I stood in front of a crowd of hundreds and tried to capture the essence of this man that I loved. This was a big job. He was SOMETHING. He was big energy, big stature, and big life. Being his partner had been one of the great honours of my life. How would I possibly capture this in a short little speech at the end of his life?

So, I stood, propped up with my crutches, took a deep breath, and this is what I said.

"I am so incredibly grateful and proud to have been Trav's wife. And just that is a testament to his life. He didn't always think before he spoke, and there was rarely a filter. At times, it seemed that he could have been just a wee bit more sensitive,

and it also appeared that perhaps he thought of himself more than others.

*And then, within the very same thought, Travis was a man who spoke light into people, was actually deeply sensitive, and put others before himself countless amounts of time. And that part, THAT is why I am so proud to have been his wife. Because he was REAL. Those who knew him would whole-heartedly agree that he was the most **genuine** person they had ever met. You got what you got.*

The night before Trav and I got married, he said to me, "Things don't go easy for me. If there is a hard way to do something, that's how it will happen for me. Are you okay to marry this?" Sweet Jesus, was he ever right! Everything was a THING. More time, more energy, more hurt feelings, more shenanigans; these were his standard operating procedures. Trav got himself into, and always somehow got himself out of, every situation imaginable.

But doing life this way taught me many things. And if you don't mind, I'd like to share a few Life Lessons that being Trav's wife taught me:

1. ***Always seek fun and adventure!***

   Travis was the fun-Master! Often, I would roll up to our driveway and literally shake my head because there was nowhere to park. The boat, the ATVs, the snowmobiles, the camper, the motorcycle. Seriously. And these things were not just for show. We really did use all of them all the time. A weekend at home on the couch was not a thing. This guy could never sit still. And this is perhaps what we all loved about him the most! He would not allow one day to go by without some sort of adventure. It wasn't just about the toys, though. He would make people laugh for literally the dumbest things. I think most of the things that I laughed the hardest at were because they were so ridiculous and not even that funny, and also so funny because he insisted they were!

- Lip-syncing songs he didn't actually know the words to
- Dancing in the kitchen with literally no rhythm and his tongue in his cheek like he was something sexy
- His constant combining of words to make one word, like fun + stupid, would be **fupid**

And then the jokes. The freaking practical jokes. There is actually an entire book worth of stories. Fake garage sales, elaborate tales, dead trees planted in the neighbour's yard, sitting through an entire hockey game exclusively speaking in Stupinsky, a language he and some buddies made up. It honestly was endless. I have never met a mind that swirled with creative and mischievous energy like his did. And that smile. That smirky smile when he knew he had you, and you were just catching on.

It was his great mission in life to instill as much fun and adventure into his own life, and the life of those around him, as possible.

2. **Eat crow**

Travis knew when he fucked up. Sometimes, it was a bit later than I would have liked, but he always eventually knew. He was never too proud to apologize and make things right.

He was the king of grand gestures to get someone's attention and apologize. And he was smart about it. He was so freaking charming, and he knew it. He used this to work his way out of any situation. But at the heart of it, always, was a desire to apologize, reconnect, and move forward.

3. **Love well**

I once made Travis read a book about Love Languages. Trav's love language was Acts of Service. The very last time I saw Trav, I was heading to Vancouver for a conference on a Thursday morning. He got up early to make sure my oil was checked before I went. Yep, out in the driveway at 6:30 am in his bathrobe and a camo toque to make sure I would be safe on my drive. This is who he was. He did ANYTHING for the people he loved.

4. ***Be strong, AND be vulnerable***

   This is perhaps what I loved the very most about Travis. Trav was the strongest man I know, probably will ever know. In every sense of the word. He literally would just pick things up and move things that did not seem humanly possible. He was the absolute rock of our family. There was nothing that the three of us girls didn't feel protected from. We could walk into and through any situation because he was with us. He had our bodies, our home, and our hearts protected. No matter what. And he made us strong. He wouldn't let us sit by and let things happen to us. He made us stand up for ourselves and what is right, make hard decisions, do things we didn't want to do, but always to make us stronger.

   And then, sigh. He would allow us to see deep into his heart and see how sensitive and vulnerable he could be with the people he trusted. Not everyone got to see that. But when you did, you knew the gift that it was. There is strength in vulnerability, and Travis showed this so, so beautifully.

5. ***Lastly, I can't talk about Trav without addressing his profound love for his daughters.***

   He loved his girls more than ANYTHING. I would constantly hear him say that the very best moment and experience of his life (and he had a lot of great ones!) was when they were born. He was so proud of who they are and are becoming. Everything he did was to provide them with the best life possible. And he did. He gave them unconditional love, safety, strength, courage, and a lifetime of incredible memories. Honestly, I don't know who has ever had more fun growing up than these two. All of these lessons that he has taught us are already in both of them, for them to continue to share with the world and keep his light shining.

6. ***One more last quick one. Go outside. Spend time outside. Just go outside.***

And then I hobbled back to my chair, listened to my brave, heartbroken daughters share their own stories about their dad, and wiped my tears.

I took it all in for the rest of the night. The stories, the tears, the dancing, the eating, the drinking, the CELEBRATION of a man who was deeply loved and was going to be incredibly missed. And then I went to bed.

How would I ever go to sleep after a night like that? Just planning that evening was the only thing that got me through the previous few weeks. It's all I could think about because it's all I *let* myself think about. So, that night in bed, I knew that this night coming to an end meant something. That was it. Now it ALL began.

My own journey with grief began with a phone call. I was out of town for a conference, and my father-in-law called me at 6:30 am to tell me that Travis was late picking him up to go hunting, and he wasn't answering his phone. He was going to our house to see what was up.

I didn't think much of it. Travis was always running late. I called him. He didn't answer. His dad called me again 20 minutes later to tell me that he had found Travis on our bedroom floor, fully dressed and unconscious. He had called 911 and was giving him CPR.

Again, to be honest, I wasn't worried. Travis had epilepsy. He would have a seizure on average about once every year and a half. I just assumed he'd had a seizure. Maybe he hit his head.

I was staying at a hotel for the conference, so I called my colleague who was staying there as well, asking her to come to my room.

When she arrived, I told her what was happening, and we collectively decided that he was going to be fine.

And then I thought, "Unconscious?" He didn't ever lose consciousness. So, I called my father-in-law back. "Did you say he was unconscious? And turning blue?"

He quickly answered "yes" and then said he had to go because the ambulance had just shown up.

He called me again about 15 minutes later. "Travis is gone."

Honestly, the next several hours are both super clear and super fuzzy.

Clear: Making the phone calls to my daughters. Picking up the phone to shatter the hearts and lives of the people you love the very most is as horrible as you think it would be.

Fuzzy: Making plans to get home and to get my daughter's home. Booking the flights, packing my things, arranging work things.

Clear: Sitting in the taxi calling his people. And my people. Trying to find the words to share what happened, and also knowing I had minimal time with them before I had to call the next person.

Fuzzy: The flight, the drive home. I think the Valium my friend gave me may have helped with this.

Clear: Pulling up to my house, looking at the front door. Knowing I was entering our home but that *everything* had changed. He wasn't going to be inside that door. He would never again greet me there.

Fuzzy: My house quickly filling with people who loved Travis and who loved me.

I do remember sitting in the living room as people were talking and thinking, "Where is Travis? He should be here. His people are in this room, and he's not here." But I don't remember the conversations. It really was like I was floating above the room just watching it all.

Clear: Lying on the floor in our bedroom in the exact spot that he had taken his last breath. I just wanted to be close to him.

The next day, my daughters decided we should get up early, hike up the mountain right behind our house, and watch the sunrise. So we did. And the sunrise was beautiful. I remember that this was a significant moment. I also know now that none of it had sunk in. We were just doing the things that made sense to do. It made sense to start our first day without him the way he would have wanted to start his day.

Coming down from the mountain, just five minutes from the top, I stepped off a rock, landed the wrong way, and *actually* heard my leg snap. ARE YOU KIDDING ME?!? I cried out in pain. But it was so much more than physical pain. All I could think of and cry out was, "Where is my husband?!? He should be here! Where is my fucking husband?!?" That was the first moment that I remember the weight of him being gone starting to set in. It wasn't just my leg that had just broken. My heart, and my whole life, had just broken. I cried out for him from the depths of my being. And my sweet daughters just stayed with me, with their own broken hearts, and watched their mom completely fall apart. It wasn't pretty.

We were at the top of the mountain, a mountain that is directly behind our house and one we had all hiked with Travis many times. It is full of steep climbs and unstable terrain. There was no chance I was walking down this mountain, so we had to wait for Search and Rescue to come and get me. While waiting, my daughter called my father-in-law (who had a whole herd of people staying at my in-laws' house). All he heard was, "Mom broke her leg, and we're on the top of the mountain." Within minutes, my 74-year-old father-in-law and a motley crew of fellow 50+ aged saviours huffed and puffed their way up the mountain to save me. Bless their hearts in their little boat shoes hiking and sweating their way to me. Eventually, they arrived— all of them—Search and Rescue and my team of heroes. After a very bumpy ride strapped to a rescue board, I was in the back of an ambulance on my way to the hospital.

Sitting in a wheelchair with my sister-in-law by my side, I was asked to fill out the paperwork for my admittance. It was pretty standard stuff until I came to the Emergency Contact part of the forms. My Emergency Contact had just died the day before. I couldn't do it. Just forming the words to say *I can't do this* was not even an option. My sweet sister took the pen from my hand and finished the job. She also made it clear to the receptionist that this was just not an ordinary broken leg or an ordinary circumstance. She insisted that it be written on my file in bold letters that my husband had died the previous day. PROCEED WITH CAUTION.

Another standard procedure for surgical patients is to remove all jewellery before they go into the operating room. This included my wedding rings. I couldn't possibly do this. Tears streamed down my face and I just shook my head no. The sweet staff understood and taped the rings to my finger. This signified to all future surgical staff that my rings be purposefully left on and, again, proceed with caution. After a surgery that included adding two rods and 13 screws to my leg, and an overnight stay at the hospital, I was heading back home again.

Breaking my leg seemed ridiculous. On top of my overwhelming emotional pain, I now had this physical pain and recovery that needed immediate attention. I was not allowed to put any weight on my leg for 6-8 weeks. So, I sat on my couch, with the incredible love and support of my family and friends, my hound dog Bernie next to me, and tried to comprehend this new reality.

I cancelled plans. A trip to Thailand for Christmas, a Fleetwood Mac concert the four of us had tickets to (which might have been equally as exciting as the trip to Thailand), and a romantic trip to Vancouver that Trav had literally planned a week prior.

And I made plans. Stupid plans. Arranging an autopsy, details with the funeral home, and planning a Celebration of Life. I wasn't interested in making ANY of these plans.

I also made plans to go back to work at the beginning of January, which would have been two and a half months after Trav died. I was hopeful that my job would be a positive distraction that would get me back into life. This didn't end up being the case. I cried every day on my way to work, sat in the parking lot and tried to gather myself, then headed in for the next few hours, and cried all the way home. I spent a lot of time staring at my computer screen, having surface conversations with my colleagues, and generally not getting a lot done. In early February, my supervisor checked in with me. She reminded me that I paid into an insurance plan that allowed me to take some paid time off and guaranteed that I'd still have my position when I got back. Given these factors, she very gently asked me why would I not take some time to heal? Duh. I couldn't really argue with that.

Looking back, I don't think the reality of losing Travis set in until January. I was focused on planning his Celebration of Life (which was freaking amazing, and SUCH a party), a trip with my daughters over Christmas break (which was pretty horrible. Good intentions. But it was so *obviously* an attempt to pretend everything was fine when it wasn't), and also healing my broken leg. In January, all of these things had passed, my daughters were back at university, and I didn't need people with me to care for me as much due to my inability to walk. All of a sudden, I was back in my "normal" life, but nothing seemed normal because Travis wasn't there.

I decided to take some additional time off work. However, I knew that I couldn't just sit at home, missing Travis. I started thinking about how I wanted to spend this time and what would be the most helpful and healing. What came together was a solo trip overseas to Greece, Jordan, Tanzania, and South Africa. With a nod to my beloved author, Elizabeth Gilbert, I coined my trip Sip, Love, Safari.

Sip: All the delicious wine in Greece and South Africa

Love: A large portion of my trip was partnering with Provision Charitable Foundation in Tanzania, supporting the work they do with people living with epilepsy. So. Much. Love.

Safari: Well, I couldn't be in Africa and not go on a safari. This was at the very top of Trav's Bucket List, and I was thrilled to do this with him in my heart.

I hesitate to share this part of my journey with other people who have experienced grief. The reason is that I recognize the PRIVILEGE in this story, and I was keenly aware of this on my trip. I worry that what I learned may not be relatable to others because not everyone has the privilege of getting the gift of time. I have come to understand that this is just my personal journey. We each have our own stories. There is no competition in grief. Nobody gets a prize for Best Griever. Well, maybe a blue participation ribbon, but nobody really likes those anyway. Grief is grief, and it hurts. There are so many ways that my heart healed on this trip, and in sharing this, my hope is that something resonates with you, and your heart connects with it, too.

Breaking my leg, and being given additional time off from my job, worked together to provide me with an extended amount of time to allow myself to dig deep into grief, and the grieving process. It helped me find some answers to relentless uncertainty and questioning:

- "How do I feel this pain fully and not sink into an abyss?"
- "Who or what can help me through this?"
- "Who am I without my husband?"
- "Will I ever feel happiness, or joy, again without the simultaneous reminder that Travis isn't here, sharing it with me?"
- "Now what?"

This journey and the days since have brought me to this place of sharing with you. I do not want my journey of healing to solely be for me. I want to share what has helped me, guided me, and continues to heal me.

*You may be interested to know the cause of Trav's death. And to be honest, so would I. After a comprehensive autopsy, the official cause of death is unknown—no heart attack, no stroke, no aneurism, not drug/alcohol-related—nothing.

REPORT CARD COMMENTS

I was a teacher for years, and I am currently a Vice Principal at a busy middle school. Because of this, I have written and read countless report cards. Because every child is precious (yes, every single one), the wording in report cards sometimes gets a bit tricky. Often there are challenges that need to be addressed, and it's important to do so with positive language.

Report card comment: Sarah is enthusiastic about sharing her opinions and thoughts.

Educators—and most parents—know that this is fluffy language for what's really going on.

Real deal: Sarah won't shut up, and she repeatedly interrupts.

Since Travis died, I've made all kinds of report card comments about him. He was amazing in many ways. He could also be a certified asshole. You know the person in your life who you often find yourself thinking, "How could they *SAY* that?!?" The one you have to warn your friends or family about before you hang out with them because you just never know what they are going to say or do.

And you find yourself wondering why you spend time with that kind of energy. AND THEN, suddenly, they do something so thoughtful, selfless and loving, that you want to keep them in your back pocket forever. That was Travis.

I spent many years feeling like I had to convince people that he wasn't an asshole—explaining things, interpreting things, reframing things, and minimizing things. Eventually,

I learned that this wasn't my job, but it took a very long time to learn this. So, when Trav died, all of a sudden, I didn't have to do this anymore. I could just talk about all his finest qualities because he wasn't pissing people off anymore. And also, I didn't want to talk about, or even think about, all of the challenges that came with loving him. It didn't seem helpful or even necessary. But to present this version of him to me and the world wasn't true to who he was.

So, this became a struggle. Talking about his faults felt uncomfortable—like I was tarnishing his legacy. Also, I didn't really want to remember those things, because remembering them was painful. Yet, I also didn't want to put him on a pedestal and pretend those parts didn't exist. So, I started creating report card comments.

RC comment: Travis chased freedom with a vengeance. He made this a priority every day.

Real deal: This was great fun when we were doing it with him. We didn't always get to join him. This didn't matter to him, and he would do his own thing whether it worked with our family or not.

RC comment: Travis pushed people to be their very best.

Real deal: He would often push his own agenda and opinion on people. Sometimes they weren't ready or willing to move forward, and he had a hard time understanding and respecting these boundaries.

RC comment: Travis was a realist.

Real deal: He would tend to see the negative aspects of things first.

RC comment: Travis was very independent.

Real deal: He could be so incredibly selfish at times.

RC comment: Travis was confident and assertive.

Real deal: He could say things that were hurtful or offensive. His intention was never to hurt someone's feelings, and yet he would, sometimes.

RC comment: Travis was strong and resilient.

Real deal: He had a difficult time with people that he perceived as "weak" and could be quite judgmental of them. He could also be quite intimidating at times.

While all of these Report Card comments are true, there's also a lot more to the story. Just as there are two sides to every coin, every quality has a positive and a negative side. Loving and living with Travis *stretched* me. One of the many lessons I learned from him was to see the strength in the things that often frustrated me. For many years, I would not have been able to even come up with report card comments about him because I was so disheartened with the real deal. I suppose this is where the beauty of marriage comes in. When perspective starts to change and gets a little wider, there's more room for love. Perspective also changes dramatically when the person who frustrated you is no longer there to do so.

So, I'll probably keep using my report card comments. I'll check myself and make an effort to ensure that his memory and legacy are true to who he really was. He would want that. He probably wouldn't want to be remembered for just his endearing qualities. He was such a button-pusher; he'd want to keep doing that even now.

GRIEF, BIG AND SMALL

C an we just talk about grief?

Not just the death-of-a-loved-one kind. Any kind of grief that leaves you undone on the couch thinking/saying/screaming, "I don't want this!" or "This is NOT what I planned!"

That's what loss does. Loss undoes our nicely planned hopes, dreams, and future, leaving us in a state with no foundation. It undoes our sense of security.

My own personal experience with grief came with the death of my husband. This was the big one and it also came in many forms prior to this.

- Driving home to six-month-old twin babies after a solo trip to the grocery store and sobbing because the idea of freedom lasting more than 20 minutes was so foreign to me it was overwhelming.

- Understanding that an important relationship to me was over, due to my own actions.

- Sitting on the couch across from my husband, agreeing that we needed to separate in order to figure us out, with tears running down both of our faces.

- Knowing my daughter was experiencing deep pain and not being able to do a single freaking thing to help her.

- Driving home from dropping off our daughters at University, being SO proud of them, while also feeling completely brokenhearted.

- And then, hobbling on crutches into a room at the funeral home, to view my beloved husband's lifeless body.

Grief comes in big doses and small doses. We're going to get both.

My plea is that we recognize this in our own journey, and the journeys of others. And offer the same kind of love, compassion, understanding, and patience that was so generously given when Travis died.

Death does not have a monopoly on grief. Grief lands on us from a wide variety of sources. Be generous with your heart. Nobody gets a pass on grief.

NOW WHAT?

I cannot count the number of times I have asked myself this in the last few years.

- Getting the news that Trav was no longer with us, Now what?

- Being on top of a mountain, not even 24 hours later, with a broken leg, Now what?

- Suddenly, becoming the owner of a business, I knew nothing about running. Irrigation contractor, Shmirrigation contractor. Now what?

- Coming home to an empty house after a long day of work, making popcorn for dinner for the third night in a row. Now what?

- Landing in Greece by myself, with an open agenda, Now what?

- Knowing I didn't ever want to get rid of our boat, and also knowing that I knew *nothing* about operating and maintaining a boat, Now what?

I actually can't even comprehend all of the Now Whats.

On October 19th, it wasn't just my husband that died. My security died, my future died, my understanding of the world died, my eternal optimism died, and my family dynamic died. And I have had to mourn each of these things. And then I have had to reconstruct each of these things. Nothing is secure. Not one little thing. Now what?

Everything I/we had planned for is no longer going to happen as I imagined. Now what?

Bad things happen. They really do. Now what?

This much-loved, larger-than-life energy source around which our family was centered was no longer here. Now what?

When your spouse dies, it changes everything—*actually* everything. The life I lived and loved with him is no longer an option. Many of the things we created together, the setting and characters of our life, remain the same. Much of my own understanding of myself and my values remains the same. Yet, everything else changes.

The question of "Now What?" encompasses every single aspect of my life.

What I have learned is that it's not helpful to think about ALL of the Now Whats. It just gets overwhelming and impossible to navigate.

What *has* been helpful is to ask myself, "What is my next step?"

What is the single next thing I need to do to get through this hour? This day?

What is the single next thing I can do to take a step toward this life without Travis?

What is one dream that I can hold on to? And then, what is one single little thing I can do to move toward that dream?

Sometimes life throws BIG things at us. And with this comes BIG emotions. The idea of navigating these curveballs and these emotions can feel like WAY. TOO. MUCH. So often, we choose to avoid the emotions or just stay in our pity pants. Neither are super helpful.

So instead, maybe just ask, "What is my next step?"

Maybe it's calling a friend, or the bank, or a repairman.

Maybe it's acknowledging your feelings and giving yourself a moment to feel them.

Maybe it's moving from your feelings to action. "Okay, self. I'm super disappointed (mad, sad, lonely), and I'm going to sit here for ten minutes and have a big, fat pity party. And then,

I'm going to mow the stupid lawn because it needs to get done, and that's something I can actually do right now."

Mowing the lawn, baking the bread, calling the realtor, Googling the question, just even getting dressed.

What's the next step?

GRIEF AND GRATITUDE

A t some point early when Trav first died, I heard this: "Gratitude keeps you from focusing on what you do not have."

I knew that if I solely focused on all of the things that I lost when Travis died, this wasn't going to help me heal. I had to balance my grief with some form of hope, and gratitude has offered me this.

Let's be real here, though. I did not/do not always feel grateful. Grief is shitty, and it's so important to feel your feels. I am not an advocate of those "Look on the bright side" or "What's the silver lining?" kind of sayings when grief has taken over, the tears are flowing, and it feels as though your heart is shattered. This is no time for a silver lining. These moments are so important to healing. However, camping out indefinitely in this place doesn't help us move forward.

Sitting on the beach in Santorini, Greece, I scribbled this into my journal:

All of this time, trying to be strong, to be brave, to grieve "well,"

Trying to make you proud,
Show that I won't crumble.

I just want you here.

I don't feel like being grateful,
Or looking for the positive,

Or being brave.

I just want you here.

Greece was hard. I was struggling with all the gratitude in my head and heart for the opportunity to be in such a beautiful place and also being so heartbroken that Travis wasn't there with me. I had never travelled alone. I had never gone to a restaurant alone. An adventure of this magnitude did not seem right without him at my side.

I'd walk the marina and find the boat he'd like the most.

I'd sit on the deck sipping coffee and imagine what our topic of conversation would be.

I'd lie in bed in my ridiculously beautiful hotel room and imagine being wrapped up in each other.

I'd sit alone in a restaurant with a cocktail and pine for him.

And then I'd head back to my room and cry myself to sleep.

I just wanted him there.

And then the very next day, I'd wake up with a heart full of gratitude—real, sincere, and deep, gratitude. I was grateful for the experience, my courage to be on this adventure on my own, his spirit within me, and I would feel lighter.

Even early on, I knew gratitude would carry me through. When the sobbing settles and the tears are drying, I have to go back to being grateful. I want to focus on what I DO have. Some days, it's the really *simple* things: my bed, my car, hot water, a cup of tea, a cute pair of shoes. Other days, it's more: my daughters' resilience, friends and family who deeply love me, a healthy body that moves and functions without difficulty. Travis and I worked hard to create a beautiful life, and although it is now missing a key factor, there is still a shit ton of beauty in my life. And Trav's no longer being here doesn't discredit all of the amazing gifts that came from my life with him. I am so grateful that we had a life together of adventures, laughter, hardship, fun, and love. I am grateful for the many lessons being his partner taught me: commitment, the importance of living in the moment, patience, loyalty, silliness, trust, the healing power of nature, and self-acceptance. I am grateful for the many lessons I have learned since his death. Every loss gives us something to learn, and for this we can be grateful.

Losing Travis has also been a huge reminder to EXPRESS love and gratitude. We really do not know what tomorrow will bring. We really don't. Being grateful helps us identify the good in our lives. It's good for our soul. It's also good for the souls of others. If you are grateful, if you are full of love for something or someone, SAY IT!

Gratitude is what has carried me through a very dark time. It has helped me focus on what is here rather than what is missing.

Gratitude has been a constant reality check for me. Yes, the love of my life is no longer here, but a lot of amazing things still are.

Gratitude helps remind me of my past and what a gift it was to have had the honour of living and learning with my husband.

Gratitude keeps me present and enjoying each moment.

Gratitude allows me to be hopeful for the future.

I think it is also important to pause here and take a moment to acknowledge what gratitude is not. It is not a rationalization in which we accept less than we deserve ("I know my boss is horrible, but I am grateful to have a job" or "I know I am not happy in my marriage, but I should be grateful for the great qualities of my husband"). It is not an excuse for complacency ("I believe that there is more for me in this life, but I need to be grateful for the things I already have"). Gratitude is not a justification for depriving ourselves of our desires ("I have been dreaming about buying this car, but it's a bit extravagant, and I should be grateful for the car I already have"). We can be grateful for what we have AND want more for ourselves.

Gratitude is a journey. Some days the road is wide, filled with beauty everywhere I look. Some days the road is narrow and strenuous. But I choose to stay on this path. I choose to continue to focus on what the Universe has blessed me with.

THE POWER OF AND

T he power of AND was first introduced to me many years ago while attending a leadership class in my Master's degree program. My professor talked about using the word "and" in place of the word "but", when offering feedback.

"You have done a great job identifying the problem, but you're stuck on the solution."

vs.

"You have done a great job identifying the problem, and it's time to focus on the solution."

See the difference?

This resonated with me, and I never forgot it. I trained myself to focus on the inclusive and positive power of AND.

Fast forward five years to the unexpected death of my husband. One of the things that surprised me while grieving was the constant barrage of contradictory feelings. In the midst of feeling the tidal wave of feelings that were coming my way, I sat down one morning and scribbled this:

I feel brave and I feel broken.

I feel love and I feel sadness.

I feel energy and freedom.

Then sorrow and loneliness.

I want my life to be a response to all of the ways,

you loved me,

stretched me,

strengthened me.

I want my response to honor you,

to make you proud.

But mostly, I want you here,

Stroking my hair,

Telling me everything will be alright.

How could I be feeling so many opposing feelings at the same time? This wondering made me dive even deeper into my love and understanding for AND.

My emotions are COMPLEX. Sometimes I feel so many things. Then I try to stop and figure out what I am *really* feeling. Where did I ever get the idea that my feelings could be contained to a one-at-a-time, first-come-first-serve, tidy little box? I started to welcome the idea that I could have opposing feelings, and it would be okay. Feelings are made for feeling. First, I have to name them; then I have to feel them. Because if I don't feel them, it's difficult to process them. If I don't process them, I don't learn from them. That's a big one. Go ahead and read those last three sentences again.

AND, became really helpful in processing my grief. It helped me create a framework for navigating my feelings. I can certainly feel this AND feel that. It is okay if these seem to be at odds with each other. In fact, learning to dance with the dichotomy has helped me become more empathetic, more flexible, and more accepting of myself and others.

Now I see this paradox of feelings all the time. Often, when I am feeling some form of tension, this is at the root.

Throughout my story, I'd like to pause to share some "and" moments along the way. My hope is that this Power of AND can show how complicated grieving is, and bring some normalcy to it. Understanding this process has been a cornerstone that I have gone back to again and again.

Gratitude *and* Longing

The moments since Trav died have created more longing in me than perhaps any other time of my life.

AND

The moments since Trav died have also created more gratitude in me than perhaps any other time in my life.

What I have learned is that these feelings are not mutually exclusive. It is possible and OKAY to be filled with gratitude for all of the beautiful things in life AND simultaneously have a deep sense of longing for what you do not have.

Losing Travis has created a longing in me that I never before experienced or understood. From the very tips of my fingers and toes and every tiny bit of me in between, I long for him. "Missing him" does not adequately capture how I feel. It's a longing that *aches* specifically for him and also for the companionship that having "a person" brings.

I dream about all of the beautiful moments that we had and those that we were supposed to have. I long for a 50th-anniversary celebration, knowing we worked our asses off to have a marriage worth celebrating. I long for sharing the swell of pride as we watch our daughters graduate from university, find their place in the world, and go after their dreams. I long for shared silence on a lazy Sunday morning in the sunshine. I even long for frustrating miscommunication. With this came knowing, that even at my worst, there is someone that knows me and loves me regardless of my flaws.

AND

I am so incredibly grateful that we created a beautiful life together. I am grateful that he chose me, that I chose him, and we continued to choose each other, over and over again.

I am filled with gratitude that our daughters are strong, resilient, compassionate human beings who are a beautiful combination of us. I am so grateful they continue to give me strength and joy when my own supply is low.

Not a day goes by that I am not overwhelmed with gratitude to my community of people. My family, my friends, my neighbors, my colleagues, people I have known for a short time, and those I have known for many, many years—they have all shown up in the most compassionate, loving, and beautiful ways. And they continue to do so.

I am grateful to live in the most stunning place. I wake up each morning to a view that continues to take my breath away, in a home that is cozy and peaceful, and a sweet dog that brings me such joy and comfort.

I am so grateful to have a job that has given me stability, joy, and a sense of purpose. This job also allowed me to take a significant amount of time off just after Trav died to grieve and heal.

My longing does not negate my gratitude. And my gratitude does not minimize my longing. They co-exist together. Some days one is greater than the other. Oddly, this brings me balance. This balance helps me be gentle with myself and others. It reminds me to be careful about jumping to gratitude before I (or others) may be ready for it. It also helps me when I am really longing, and wanting, and *begging* for something. I can be confident that I will get to the gratitude. Maybe not in that moment, but it will come. I just need a little patience and trust.

WHEN MOVING ON FEELS LIKE MOVING AWAY

M oving on. Getting over it. Getting past it.

Ugh.

I have deeply struggled with this. Early on, someone shared with me a TedTalk by Norah McInerny (of *Hot Young Widows Club*) that beautifully captures the notion of moving forward rather than moving "on" from loss. This was super helpful in navigating my future without Travis. But I struggle with moving forward, too. In so many ways, moving forward equates to moving away from Travis. So even moving forward in a healthy way was extremely challenging for me to wrap my head around.

The day Travis died, I decided to sleep on his side of the bed, so I could be as close to him as possible. I also decided that I was never going to wash my sheets again. Mmmhmm. But I was committed. On night four, I woke up to go to the bathroom. I was doped-up on Tylenol 3s after my surgery, and in case you are fortunate enough to NOT know what these do to your bowels, let's just say I had some trouble "getting things moving." I woke up with some rumblings of "movement" and knew I needed to pay attention. Sigh. This was not a simple task. Remember the broken leg? I had to finagle my way to my crutches, hobble to the bathroom, and then *whoomp* down on the toilet. Nothing. Not even a rabbit turd. Back I hobbled to bed. Ten minutes later, more rumblings. Crutches, hobbling, whoomp...one freaking rabbit turd. ONE! Back to bed. Ten minutes later, I WISH I WAS KIDDING! Well, this time, I had success—maybe too much success—as I hobbled back to bed feeling satisfied that perhaps I could now get some sleep. I got my leg up onto the mountain of pillows that were keeping it elevated and noticed something wet on the bed. Are you kidding me? My last mission to the bathroom had been so successful that I "succeeded" all over my leg, and it was now all over the sheets. THE SHEETS THAT I WAS NEVER GOING TO WASH!!! I literally shit the bed.

Right or wrong, but I grabbed the towel that was on my bed, laid it over my mess, and cried myself to sleep.

Washing my sheets the next day was my first step in moving forward. I was not happy about it. I'm still not happy about moving forward. But each day continues to come.

Often, moving forward feels like moving away from Trav. I want to hold on to every little piece of him. And I struggle with knowing how to hang on to him and not get stuck.

While on my Sip, Love, Safari trip, I spent some time in Jordan.

On my last day there, I spent some time at the Dead Sea. And no, the irony is not lost on me. I remember sitting on a lounge chair and watching the sun set. Everything about this moment oozed Travis: boats on the water catching the magic of the evening, people flying in little self-propelled helicopter things that he would have loved renting, the palm and banana trees, and even the irrigation pipes sticking out of the ground. I remember very vividly a shift taking place. It was the very first time that I felt him nudge me towards letting go. It was the first time that I felt like I could hear his audible voice in my head. And he was telling me to LIVE and the importance of finding happiness without him here. It brought such a sense of peace and then deep sadness. I started to cry, *really* cry, while I was still on the lounge chair. A lovely little couple was next to me, pretending not to notice that the woman next to them was falling apart. Bless their hearts.

And then, and I'm not kidding you, a rainbow appeared. And I remember thinking, even considering my shattered heart, that perhaps some beauty would one day come from this shit storm I was living in. It didn't have to mean letting go—maybe it could mean a new adventure. With him in my heart, rather than by my side.

Holding on *and* Letting Go

This is a hard one.

There are many things that are worth holding on to and are important to hold on to—family, creativity, hobbies, faith, memories.

There also comes a time when it is necessary and healthy to let go of something: a relationship, expectations, an apology that will never come.

What about when what feels right and healthy is to hold on AND let go, all at the same time?

I am coming to a place in my grief journey where both of these are feeling right.

Initially, the only thing that kept me from sinking was holding on. Holding tight to the feel of Travis lying next to me in bed, his voice, his laugh, his touch. Smelling his clothes, lying on his side of the bed, sitting in his chair, holding his things. All of these actions kept him close and made his absence a little less painful.

The idea of letting go would make me angry and fearful. Holding on meant I didn't have to let go. And letting go meant I could no longer hang on.

These days, I am beginning to see it a bit differently.

I am starting to understand that I can hold on to the love, to us, to the memories, to the ways he helped me stretch and grow, AND I can start to let go of having him here on this earth.

I am learning that the essence of Trav—his adventure, his courage, his tenderness, his passion for life—is no longer in his physical body. It is now within the people he loved most. In many ways, this allows for me to be close to him in ways that were not even possible while he was here on earth. This gives me 24/7 access. This gives me access to all the best parts of him without the frustrating parts mucking things up.

Because of this, I can hold on AND let go. Both of these seem right and healthy.

This understanding creates a curiosity in me. Where else in my life can I hold tight and let go?

Particular dreams—maybe I can hold tight to the essence or idea behind it and let go of the specific way I imagined it would manifest.

Relationships—maybe I can hold on to the important lesson(s) I learned from somebody and let go of the expectation that our friendship will continue to look like it always has.

This process includes A LOT of emotions. Just the words "letting go" often bring tears and deep breaths. And "holding on" in some odd way brings some shame and regret.

So, I keep coming back to the AND. It's okay to feel both at the same time.

Holding on and letting go. It's a process.

WHAT DOES GRIEVING WELL MEAN ANYWAY?

W hen I made a commitment to myself that I was going to "grieve well," I truly had no idea what that even meant. I recognized early on that there was no right or wrong way to grieve, so how could I commit to doing it well? I knew that I didn't want to look back several years down the road and see that losing Travis had ruined me. I didn't want to get stuck in a place of bitterness or hopelessness. I wanted to make sure that I did every possible thing to process this loss in a healthy way. It quickly became clear that a critical aspect in doing so was to give myself permission to feel all of my feelings. I did not want to stuff them away and hope they didn't show up later. Also, I have never been a stuffer of emotions. I've tried, but it never ends up pretty. So, when the feelings came, I let them sweep over me, or crash over me. And there have been some serious moments of *feelings*.

In retrospect, I'm actually pretty disappointed with my reaction to finding out that Travis had died. It's probably a bit morbid (but I'm hoping a bit normal) that I had thought about that moment before. When Travis would be off on one of his adventures, when we spent time apart, or when I was feeling especially close with him, the question of "What would I ever do if he died?" would cross my mind. And I would conjure up dramatic moments of me falling on the floor, screaming "Noooo" or "Whhhhy?" and wailing uncontrollably.

In reality, when Trav's dad called and told me he had died, my response was, "Okay, thank you for letting me know. I'll call you later."

And when his sister first called moments later to see how I was, my response was, "Well, my husband is dead. So, there's that."

What?!?!? Really, Heidi? That's all I had?

Don't worry. I get it. I was in shock. My mind just wasn't able to process what was happening. I just wish I'd had a better response. At least, a *different* response.

It caught up. I remember having a complete meltdown one evening when I wanted to watch a movie and couldn't get the remote control to work. And I couldn't just walk away because my freaking leg was broken. And I was so mad at Travis for leaving me with THREE remote controls to the same TV with no explanation as to which did what. Why do we need three?!? So, I hopped out of the room (literally hopped!), hobbled up the stairs, threw myself onto my bed, and cried myself to sleep.

On my Sip, Love, Safari trip, I woke up early one morning in Zanzibar, Tanzania. I could see the sun rising on the beach from my bed. It was stunning. Waking up alone in an incredibly romantic setting crashed over me, and my body physically ached for Travis. I later wrote about this moment, saying,

"This morning was messy. Ugly cry, fetal position messy. I didn't want to be brave, or grateful, or positive. I just wanted Travis here. I moved through it and then took myself out for a cup of tea and stared out at this most beautiful view. And then I felt brave, grateful, and positive."

What I realized is that it's about living each moment. It's okay to FEEL my feels in each moment—even if those feelings are a juxtaposition. Grief does not have to be exclusive. And neither does gratitude. Yet, it's important to understand that every moment is just that. Moments pass. Good and bad, they pass.

What I learned was if I allowed myself to really feel my emotions, it didn't take long for them to pass. I came to trust that I didn't have to feel every aspect of my grief all at once;

I just had to feel what was showing up at that moment. My body knew what I was capable of handling and processing in that moment, and I could trust that I would just deal with that particular emotion. All of the other feelings would have their time. Sometimes the feelings have been overwhelmingly strong, and other times not so much. But I can trust that whatever they are, if I give them expression, they will pass. On the contrary, if I don't express them, they will build. And they will still show up, just not in ways that necessarily make sense.

The second Christmas after Travis died, I went with my daughters and another couple to Costa Rica. I was determined we were going to have FUN, and this wasn't going to be a vacation that focussed on the loss of Travis. Two days in, and the grief wave was building. I persisted in my insistence to have FUN, damn it. I didn't want my girls to see me upset, so I really tried to convince myself that I was okay. By day four, I was getting bitchy about the money we were spending, how their time was being spent, and all of the tiny things that didn't actually matter to me. I was making myself, and perhaps all of the others, miserable. So, I asked them to go out for dinner without me that night. I stayed home and reverted back to the ugly cry. I moaned and wailed, cried, and writhed. And then I felt better.

When we ignore our pain, it just gets bigger. When we feel it, it doesn't disappear, but it becomes manageable. And we can respond to it in such a way that helps us learn and grow from it.

HERE'S WHAT
TRULY HELPS

P eople don't know what to do when someone dies. So they cook. And they bake. And then you have a freezer full of food for one person.

I *know* that these good people just want to do something to help. They want to do *something* to let you know they care about you, are thinking about you, and want to make things just a tiny bit easier. But, sweet ones, the freezer full of food really did not make a dent in the gut-punch of losing my husband.

The first few days after Travis died, my house was FULL of people—people who loved Travis, loved the girls and me, and wanted to be close. I don't think these lovely beings knew what to do with themselves while they were here. And to be honest, I didn't really know what to do with them being here, either!

One of those mornings, I looked out my living room window and saw my mom on her hands and knees in my front flower bed. She was weeding, trimming, and getting my garden ready for winter. Her husband had a bucket of soapy water and the vacuum out there detailing Travis's truck. I will never forget these acts of love. I was two days into losing my husband, and I had a broken leg. Those chores they were doing needed to get done, and I sure as shit wasn't going to do them. *These* are the things that people dealing with acute grief desperately need and greatly appreciate.

I know people don't know what to do or what to say. I really do know that people want to help lessen the pain, and so often, they just feel helpless. Here is a list of some helpful things people did for me when I was grieving: [1]

- Fixed the water filter in my fridge
- Sent me texts regularly letting me know they were thinking about me and explicitly said there was no expectation for a response
- Helped me fill out paperwork for the funeral director
- Sent me a love note in the mail every month for the first year
- Visited three to five times a week for six weeks to provide laser treatment on my leg to ensure it healed properly
- Drove me to physiotherapy appointments, waited in the lobby, and drove me back home
- Asked me about Travis. "Tell me a story about the time…"
- Called me around bedtime to say goodnight
- Didn't ask what they could do to help plan his celebration of life—they just did it
  - "I'm going to put a slide show together; can you send some pictures?"
  - "I'm ordering the items from the rental store; how many chairs do you think we need?"
  - "I can pick up the food. What time will it be ready?"
- Took my dog for a walk
- Made an appointment for a massage, let me know the date, and took me there
- Vacuumed the house
- Came for a visit, brought lunch with them, cleaned up, and then left. Total visit time: 1 hour
- Remembered important dates: Our anniversary, his birthday, the anniversary of his death and made certain to acknowledge these dates

To help you out, here are the common themes:

Don't ask, "What can I do?" Think of what is needed, and just do that.

Don't feel that you have to say the right thing. There is *nothing* you can say that will make it better—nothing—just acknowledge.

Talk about their person. Please don't be afraid to do this.

Put that in your notes. Unfortunately, it will come in handy one day.

PATIENCE AND TRUST

I t's a funny thing moving forward. I feel like this grief should have lifted by now. Perhaps it's not quite as heavy on a minute-by-minute basis as it once was, but it is still so incredibly present. Grappling with feeling like this is likely normal, but so wanting to be further along this journey. Missing him and wanting him close while simultaneously wanting to move forward and not have this weight be so heavy anymore.

I have spent much time over the last little while wrestling with a million versions of the above paragraph. I've been frustrated that the process isn't moving as quickly as I would like. And then I'm frustrated that I'm frustrated! My mind understands that grief is a process, a journey that doesn't have a detailed map with an estimated arrival date. My heart just hasn't really settled into this belief. The phrase "patience and trust" is the title track in this journey, and I have returned to it numerous times a day. It has become a rock that grounds me and brings me back into focus. I am beginning to take comfort in being patient with the process and trusting both myself and this journey.

I am also learning to have patience and trust with this emerging version of myself. I've spent a lot of time trying to figure out who I am without Travis here. I met Trav when I was 21. Just a baby! So much of my own self-discovery has been influenced by him. So much of my time and identity was wrapped up in him. So who am I now that he isn't here? And how do I even begin to figure this out?

Losing him has often felt like losing a piece of myself. Losing this kind of love, both giving and receiving it, is a piece of my heart that will never return. And parts of myself that I have always loved feel lost as well. My innocent, free-spirited, positive, and easy-breezy self seems nowhere to be found. It feels like who I was will never be again. And I liked who I was. I wonder if this deep sadness that has become my baseline will always remain. Will true joy ever return?

Patience and trust—*trusting* that I will discover new aspects of myself through this journey; and *being patient* while I grow into a different version of myself—a version that is true to who I have always been, but also has room to discover new aspects of growth and depth.

So often, when I lose sight of patience and trust, I get overwhelmed and almost anxious about "finding myself" and this process of discovering who I am. I feel as if, when I get there, I will find my purpose and the meaning behind this journey. THEN I will be able to move forward—THEN I won't feel so much pain—THEN so many questions will be answered. The other day, while walking my dog, and deep in this process, I stopped. I realized that I am spending so much time and energy trying to figure out who I am and who I am is *RIGHT HERE.*

I am...

Strong

Vulnerable

Messy

Heartbroken

Empathetic

Resilient

Real

Brave

And then there's another aspect of Patience and Trust.

One of the unexpected surprises that has come from this last year and a half is the possibility for growth that lies before me. I find myself in a position where there really aren't any boundaries. And I've spent so much time dreaming about what might be in my future.

If this is my life now, what do I want it to look like? I've dreamed up some pretty great plans. And I'm excited to see them come to fruition (Hello! Writing this book!)

There are many things that are in my future, AND there are many things that are in my present. I am learning to focus on this present day, listen to myself, and move forward with what feels right today.

This conflicts with the part of me that just wants to skip ahead. I want to skip to a day when I have become comfortable with missing Travis and having him close in a way that doesn't break my heart daily.

I want to skip to a time when I can feel immense joy without the side pain of wishing Trav was here to experience it with me.

I want to skip to a day when my dreams of sharing love and compassion with the world are being manifested in a meaningful way.

I want to skip to living in the *meaning* I have found through Trav's death, and not just the mourning.

It's such a journey, this whole thing of life. And what is keeping me on track, what I repeat to myself daily, perhaps hourly, is Patience and Trust.

Be patient with the process and with myself. Trust both the process and myself.

If I am *really* paying attention. If I am doing the work of really living through each day. If I am listening to myself and responding to the next right thing. If I am committed to this day, and then the next, as they come. If I am responding to the creative nudges that speak to me. Then, I will get to where I am supposed to be.

I have to trust this journey and all of the little journeys along the way. I need to trust that I am getting there. However long it may take. I am getting there.

Every day, every hour: Patience and Trust.

FOUR-LEGGED FRIEND

When my father-in-law got to our house on the day Travis died, he found our dog, Bernie, sitting right by Trav's side. As the paramedics worked on Travis, Bernie paced back and forth throughout the house. He knew.

For many months after Trav died, Bernie was definitely out-of-sorts. It took us a while to find our groove as a duo rather than a trio. I wish I could say that he just knows when I'm having a bad day and comes to give me snuggles. He doesn't.

But it reminds me that I still have to actually ask for what I want. Even if I'm asking it from a dog, who doesn't even understand English. Whatever.

I regularly ask myself, "What would I do without this sweet dog?"

He keeps me company.

He keeps me getting up each morning.

He keeps me dedicated to getting outside every day.

He sits beside me on my bad days.

He keeps me playful.

He listens to me when I just have to talk out loud to figure out my thoughts.

He is an outlet for all this love I still have in me that has nowhere to go.

And I am SO GRATEFUL for him.

I'm not saying it's IMPOSSIBLE to grieve without a dog to love, but I wouldn't suggest it.

CHANGE THE OIL

I have a picture of Travis on my nightstand that I unknowingly took the very last time I saw him. It's a reminder to me of how well I was loved and also to love others in this same way.

On that last morning together, Travis got me up early. It had been a busy week, and we hadn't had much time to connect with each other. I was heading out of town that day after work for the weekend, and Travis wanted to make sure we had some time to just be together. So he woke me up a half-hour earlier than normal and, while I got ready for the day, he made us coffee. We sat on the couch and shared about our week, discussed what was coming up, and sat together enjoying each other's company.

As mentioned, I was going out of town. So, when we were done with our coffee, he headed outside in his bathrobe and camouflage toque on a cold October morning to check the oil in my car. He wanted to make sure I was good to make the five-hour drive ahead of me.

When he was done, we kissed goodbye, and off I went. That was the last time I ever saw him.

There are a couple of important lessons here that Travis taught us all on that morning:

1. Make time for connection. Even when we think we don't have the time, make it. Make the coffee, pour the wine, go for the walk, make the phone call, schedule the time, put your phone down. Do what you need to do to make the time to connect with the ones you love.

2. Show your people you love them. Don't just say it—show it. In whatever ways make sense and mean the most.

Change the oil, write a note, leave a little something where they'll find it, invite them to spend some uninterrupted time together, hold their hand, clean the house, whatever it is. Do the things that communicate how much you love and appreciate them. Make them feel special. Let them know that you are thinking about them and are so grateful to get to love them.

Love your people this way—your partner, your children, your friends, your parents, and your dog. Celebrate love like this on important days and regular days. It will make each day sweeter, and you just never know if those moments will come again.

CHOOSING GROWTH

Pain and heartache are inevitable. We *will* experience them, and nobody gets a pass. We are then faced with a couple of options: We can either choose to get stuck in the pain, or we can learn and grow from it. I choose growth.

Choosing growth isn't necessarily the easiest option. In Glennon Doyle's book *Untamed* (if you've been under a rock and haven't read it, please do. It is so good. Go get yourself a copy!), one of her key messages is We Can Do Hard Things. Amen to this! What I love about this is that "hard things" are different from person to person and day to day. They are big steps and little steps.

My grief story with Trav includes a lot of hard things, and many of them started way before October 19th, 2018. Because my grief story began with a love story, and once a love story gets past the initial starry-eyed, fairy tale beginnings, shit gets real.

After about twelve years of marriage, we started to struggle—and not the little struggles of parenting fatigue like *who-left-the-socks-on-the-floor* or *it's-not-my-turn-to-empty-the-dishwasher* variety. I'm talking about the *I might hate you more than I love you, do we even want to be married* kind. I had started teaching and was no longer available as much as I once had been. We were struggling financially, and we both found ourselves in our own journeys of self-discovery. Travis felt inadequate, and I fueled this flame. So we drifted, and we put up walls, and we stopped seeking the best for each other and began to focus on what was best for ourselves. This went on for a couple of years.

This eventually led to a tearful, heartbreaking conversation that ended in the decision to separate. Honestly, neither Travis nor I knew where this was going to lead. We weren't making definite plans for divorce; we just knew that we simply could not keep going the way things were. To be honest, I had to really wrestle with whether or not I felt I would be "okay" on my own. Could I do this life without him? (Well that's some foreshadowing!) Eventually, my answer to this was yes. I loved Travis, and I was also not willing to stay in a marriage that was making us both miserable.

So, we went to work. We sorted out who would live where. Trav went to therapy. I went to therapy. We went to therapy together.

We had hard conversations and heard things that were both painful to hear and necessary to hear. And then, I woke up one morning to an email he had sent late the night before. The letter absolutely bared his soul. All the things I had wanted to hear for years, he said. All the things that had hurt my heart, he acknowledged. All the questions I had, he answered.

I got these emails every single morning for a week straight. And my broken heart started to mend a little. His broken heart started to mend a little. The walls began to come down, the tenderness started to return, and the mending began.

All of these hard conversations continued, but a few things changed:

1. We stopped keeping score.
2. We stopped looking back and started looking forward.
3. We were no longer interested in changing each other. We just focused on our own work.

And we made it back to each other with a SHIT TON of sweat, and tears, and commitment. We did this really hard thing together.

And then, three years later, he died.

Just when we had made it. We had raised our daughters and proudly watched them head off into the world. We had bought our dream home and made it our own. Travis was what he liked to call "pre-tired" and working minimal hours. And we REALLY liked each other. We really were in love all over again. We had this whole, beautiful life in front of us.

This is where it all seems so unfair. We DID THE WORK, and this is what I got? This is where my heart breaks with all of the unmet plans, all of the dreams unlived, and all of the ways I don't get to reap the rewards for our hard work.

So, I got a whole new list of hard things:

- Selling my husband's business
- Clearing out the garage and going through all of Trav's things that brought him so much joy
- Figuring out how to balance chemicals in the hot tub
- Calling the mechanic to get snow tires put on my car
- Organizing a Celebration of Life for Travis while nursing a broken leg on our couch
- Shovelling the snow off the driveway
- Sitting by myself at restaurants

To an outsider, some of these may be big and overwhelming. Some of these may seem small and manageable. But each one of these tasks was incredibly difficult for me. Each one brought me to tears and left me saying, "I can't do this."

After returning from my Sip, Love, Safari trip, I had a whole day of hard things. I was just coming back from an adventure of a lifetime. It was painful, and it was also amazing. It was definitely hard to come back to reality. Especially the reality of my "regular" life without Trav in it. I was frustrated that I couldn't retain the high of my trip. And then frustrated at my frustration because I knew this wasn't reality. All of my adventurous, positive, powerful vibes were nowhere to be found. I didn't feel like meditating, being grateful, or even allowing myself to feel hope.

Doing the yard work, buying hanging baskets (that Travis would have gotten me for Mother's Day), cleaning the boat, power washing the deck all overwhelmed me with grief. All of these were Trav's jobs, and it was abundantly clear that he was no longer here. Not only did my heart miss him, but my LIFE missed him.

I remember feeling defeated. I just gave up trying to be strong and broke down sobbing. I recall actually lying down on the couch and pounding my fists. These were not difficult tasks. And they left me undone.

Pause.

AND accomplishing each one of these things (and countless more) made me stronger. Each time I did something I didn't want to do or thought I couldn't do, it made me more confident in my ability to do hard things.

What I have learned from doing hard things is that I am:

- Stronger than I ever knew
- More knowledgeable about taxes, and probate, and accountant foreign language than I ever dreamed I'd be
- Able to make space for feeling my emotions, AND still get shit done
- Enjoying my own company
- Capable of learning new skills, even ones I'm not really interested in learning

I have also figured out that:

- Courage breeds courage. Every time I do something hard, the next hard thing is just a wee bit easier
- Courage is also contagious. As I build my brave heart, it encourages others to do the same.
- Feeling proud of yourself is a very good feeling

We have to grunt if we want to grow. The grunting is so incredibly hard, and the growth is so incredibly beautiful.

THE TWINS

During our last summer together as a family of four, we bought a boat. We had just moved to a region of British Columbia on the gorgeous Okanagan Lake, and Travis was set on spending as much time together as possible before our girls headed off to university. His logic was that if we had a boat, this would mean more time together. I fell for it.

It turned out to be true. We spent HOURS on the boat that last summer. And I can say with absolute certainty that that summer was the best of our lives—for all four of us. It was one of those magical times when, right in the midst of it, you knew it was special. Each day we would wake up and take our dog for a walk, decide if we were going for a hike or playing tennis, make lunch, and then head out on the boat. The girls would join us after work, and we'd cruise, surf, swim, and watch the sunset. I vividly remember thinking that I felt like a teenager when she gets a boyfriend, and her friends wonder where she went. It was that good.

I also remember thinking how grateful I was that after all these years together, there was nobody I would rather spend my days with. Some days we would go for a hike and talk the entire time, and other days we would say very few words. And both were beautiful. We truly just enjoyed each other's company.

When the next summer came around, and he was no longer here, I didn't know how I would possibly get back on that boat. And I *really* didn't know how I would possibly take care of all the responsibilities that come with owning a boat.

And this is where my girls saved me. My smart, independent, strong, and beautiful girls who were grieving the BEST DAD stepped up and gave me the strength that I needed. Getting back on that boat was non-negotiable for them. I did not want to do it. I didn't think I'd be able to handle it. Nobody even knew how to drive the freaking thing. And there was no option but to do it.

I just have to take a moment to go back to that "BEST DAD" part. Our family did it all—camping, boating, hiking, fishing, skiing, ATVing, roasting hot dogs by a bonfire in the snow— all the fun. This was because of Travis. He wasn't going to stop his adventures because he became a parent. The girls became part of the gig. And this gave them so, so much— a love of the outdoors, an understanding that things don't always go as planned, the security in knowing that their dad wanted them with him on these adventures, and not being afraid to get a little dirty. This also instilled in them perseverance, grit, and an understanding that sometimes you just have to put your head down and get shit done without complaining. If they were cold, put another jacket on. If they were tired, just keep going. If they were bored, make up a game. They both have a deep reservoir of memories filled with being outside and learning to love all of the things that go along with the outdoors.

The day we put the boat back in the water was a shit show. One of the tires on the trailer nearly fell off, the plug for the boat was discovered to be missing while we were backing the boat into the boat launch (it turns out this is a VERY important little piece of the boat), and the boat overheated about 15 million times. For the Love of the Lord. Of course, all of these things happened. Of course, it wasn't going to be easy.

And then we finally got on the water. And Fleetwood Mac started playing. And Kendra started surfing. And Jenna hugged me tightly (a gesture that, in itself, is a miracle from the heavens!) And I knew I could do it. I would learn to drive that boat, maintain that boat, and boat *the shit* out of that boat!

On that boat, on that day, my daughters gave me the greatest gift. They reminded me that joy could return. And it was a 'deep in my heart,' *feel it in my toes* kind of joy. And the adventurous and life-giving spirit of Travis was very much alive and here to stay. Travis's determination and will to keep going, no matter what, was deeply embedded in the DNA of our beautiful daughters. They are his gift to me for always. To remind me of him, to remind me of us, to remind me that I can do it. Whatever it is.

Also, you should see me drive the boat now. I kick ass.

THOUGHTS ON GOD

"Use your heart, and you will see God in all human beings."
- *unknown*

I found this quote while in Mahenge, Tanzania. This is a small village that has one of the highest rates of epilepsy in the world. I went to see how I could help—silly me. What I experienced there was the closest experience to God I can imagine and the closest to God I have ever been.

I grew up in a Christian home. My earliest memories of Sunday mornings are heading off to church as a family in our blue Buick. I learned the Sunday school songs and memorized the Bible verses. Sing it with me, "Father Abraham had seven sons, and seven sons had Father Abraham..."

As a teenager, I continued to be a good "Christian" girl. I had nice friends, I didn't party, I went to youth group every Tuesday night, and I did my best to wake up most mornings for "Quiet Time" with Jesus.

My first really serious boyfriend became my husband. I "saved" myself for him because that was the "right" thing to do. I don't mean I waited until I got married to have sex, because we didn't. I was three months pregnant at our wedding. And, looking back, there was a whole lot of shame in telling our friends and family that I was pregnant BEFORE we got married. Gasp.

When our girls were little, we would still bundle up and head off to church most Sundays. This time was in a grey minivan.

And then, somewhere along the way, things stopped making sense. All of the stories I had grown up with started to feel flat. I began to question all of the rules and the "shoulds". As time went on, we stopped going to church, my questioning increased, and pretty soon, I found myself not really knowing what I believed anymore. To be more accurate, I DID know what I did not believe. And mostly, it was all of the things I had held so tightly to as a "good Christian."

I was okay with not really believing anything. I didn't believe I needed a definitive outline of what I did and did not believe to be true. Whatever.

And then my husband died. I remember, shortly after he died, considering heaven. There were so many words of comfort that were based on "He is in a better place" or "You'll see him again one day." And I remember thinking it was all horseshit. All that mattered to me, all that seemed real, was that he wasn't *here*, with me.

At the same time, I sure didn't like the idea that he was just dead. I thought about this a lot. A LOT.

And then one day I was driving, with four hours ahead of me until I was home, and I decided it would be a good time to try listening to a podcast. Of course, the obvious starting point in my podcast journey was with Oprah.

She was talking to Bradley Cooper (Swoon!) about the death of his father. This is what Oprah said:

"I believe that when somebody who loves you here in this dense plane, when they pass, the energy of them abides with you in a way that it absolutely could not have when they were in their dense body. That something happens in the transference. The spirit of that person comes in and abides with you in a way that was not possible on the earth plane."

Well, now I nearly needed to pull over because I was sobbing. **THIS** made sense to me. In an effort to pull myself together, I turned on the radio as a distraction.

Quick side story: Travis and I were just friends for several months before we started dating. He had made it clear that he was interested in more, and I had made it clear that we were just friends. For his birthday, he had asked me if I would go to his hometown with him for the weekend. I agreed, and off we went on the four-hour journey. Trav popped in a mixed tape (remember those?), and Tracy Chapman's "Fast Car" came on. There he was, window rolled down, music blaring, and singing along to the song (very loudly and VERY off-key). I looked at him, and in an instant, I thought, "Oh, dear God, I'm in love with him!" This moment, and everything about it, burned itself into my memory. The weekend ended with "the talk," some kissing, and him officially becoming my boyfriend.

You may see where this is going.

So, I turn the radio on to distract myself from my Oprah moment, my tears, and my new understanding of how powerfully Travis can remain with me.

Of course, "Fast Car" is playing. There's more.

People! The song was playing, and I was driving in the EXACT location as it all happened 23 years before. The same freaking spot!

And so began my curiosity, and reexamination, of God.

I am most definitely still on a journey in this area. Currently, I like to refer to what most people call God, as Spirit. I felt like a 'renaming' was necessary to get past all of the baggage and misunderstandings from my previous experience with God. And also, because I am coming to a new understanding of Spirit.

Spirit celebrates you. Just as you are, no expectations. Just simply *being* is worth celebrating.

Spirit is FULL of joy. When I let go of all the things and experience the love of Spirit, there is deep, unabashed joy.

Spirit is about love, not about rules and expectations. Spirit is about being connected to Spirit, this earth, and its people. Period.

Spirit does not rank people. As far as Spirit is concerned, the wealthy, the poor, the organized, the messy, the proper, the edgy, the clean, and the dirty are all full of BEAUTY.

Spirit is interested in ME. Spirit doesn't really want me to worry about what message others are receiving.

When I was in Mahenge, this is the Spirit that I felt within me, within the people I met, and all around me.

This, I am interested in.

NEAR AND FAR

R emember that Sesame Street™ episode with Grover demonstrating Near and Far?

With his friendly eyes and pink nose right up close to the camera, and in his gravelly, sweet monster voice, he clearly announces, "Near!"

And then he wobbles his furry blue body away to the far end of the room and declares "Far!" in a muffled yell.

For an Eighties child like me, this is a very familiar image.

And it's a great representation of how I'm feeling these days. As I write this, the anniversary of Trav's death is quickly approaching. * And I'm feeling frustrated because, more than anything, I want to feel close to him, to help me through these next couple of weeks. Instead, he's feeling pretty far away.

When Trav first died, he felt RIGHT THERE. I could still smell him on his clothes in our closet, feel his body imprint in our bed, hear his laugh, sense his spirit in the garage with all of his treasures. All of these things are feeling pretty far away these days.

Of course, there are also living memories of him that keep him near:

...In my daughters. My beautiful reminders of his physical presence. It's almost eerie how much Jenna looks like him, and our girl Kendra was blessed with those eyes! And also in the way his spirit is so alive in both of them; his sense of adventure, his slightly inappropriate sense of humour (Report card comment alert! The real deal is that his was more than "slightly" inappropriate), his love of the outdoors, his loyalty to those he loved, his drive and work ethic, his inability to focus on one particular thing for an extended amount of time.

...in this beautiful home I live in, that he worked so hard to complete.

...in my own need for adventure, seemingly embedded in me in ways that are more profound than when he was here.

...and in the way that the people he loved continue to love me so well.

And yet, I'm still left feeling unsettled that he is feeling pretty far away.

Then a cherished friend of mine reminded me that relationships are full of ups and downs. In his life here on earth, I often felt super close to Trav. And sometimes pretty far away—even when we were lying on the couch together just a foot apart. This is a normal part of relationships.

He is no longer here on this earth, and yet still, the essence of our relationship continues to live on. Sometimes he's near. Sometimes he's far.

Oddly, this familiarity has brought me comfort in this new relationship with him that I now find myself navigating.

Near *and* far. With this adorable monster of mine.

*Can someone please invent a proper word for this sort of day? Anniversary? Come on. Not really something to celebrate. Dead day? Fitting, but a bit much. How has an appropriate term for this not been invented yet? It's a day to be remembered. It definitely deserves recognition and a title. I've yet to hear a good one, though.

IT'S OK TO STILL FEEL AFRAID

I am fearful of a lot of things.

- My house will fall apart because I don't know how to fix all of the things
- My children won't feel the total weight of parental love with Travis not here
- Mice
- Going on a date and having a good time
- I will no longer have any real fun without Trav here
- Making a wrong financial decision
- Disappointing someone I love
- Hurting someone's feelings
- Missing an opportunity because I make being comfortable a priority
- Looking fat, or old, or some other bullshit women are led to believe is the unforgivable

AND

I am learning how to fix things, and it's also okay to pay someone to help me.

I will continue to love my daughters with everything I have and trust that they will have their own continued connection with Travis.

I set a mouse trap and disposed of a MASSIVE wood rat, and I also fished a dead mouse out of my pool (Well, my neighbor did. But close enough.)

I'm making small mental steps toward being okay with the possibility of a date one day.

I consciously make plans to include adventure and fun regularly in my life.

I can trust professionals to offer guidance and support with my money.

I trust that when (not if) I do disappoint someone, we can talk about it, and I can give and receive understanding.

I trust that hurting someone's feelings is never my intention and, when it happens, I can have a mature conversation that may or may not need an apology.

I am taking risks to include more creativity and vulnerability.

I wear my bathing suit without a cover-up, wear shorts that just might be a bit "too" short, and I am learning to love my body as it is.

Here's what I'm getting at: Just because I am afraid of something doesn't mean I get to avoid it. I can be steeped in fear and muster up the courage to take one small step. Or maybe even a big, huge freaking step. Courage and fear can happen at the exact same time. In fact, if you're not a little bit afraid, courage isn't needed.

Fear doesn't have to stop us.

It's okay to be afraid. But I don't want fear to keep me from living the truest, most beautiful life possible for me.

Doing scary things requires courage and builds resilience, confidence, and trust.

And who doesn't want those?

GRACE IS THE FOUNDATION

Nothing brings to light who you really are more than grief. I have heard it said that when a person is grieving, the essence of who they are is only magnified. Who you are at the core comes shining through, whether you like it or not. You can't hide it.

When grieving alongside people you love, you begin to notice that there are many ways of expressing grief.

My own personal experience with grief—and grieving alongside the many people who deeply felt Trav's loss—showed me how personal grieving is. The expression of grief depends on the circumstances of loss, the relationship with the person that died, and the personality of the one who is grieving. As the people in my own circle grieved the loss of Travis (husband, father, brother, son, friend), each expression of grief was completely unique:

- Talking about our feelings, and not talking about our feelings.
- Crying and keeping our feelings to ourselves.
- Needing space and needing to be close.
- Taking time "off" from life and putting ourselves right back into our daily grind.
- Keeping busy and slowing down.

None of these were right, and none of these were wrong. We had to give each other space and understand that even though someone else's grief didn't look like our own, it wasn't wrong. It was what they needed.

This way of thinking began to broaden itself outside of the realm of grief. I started to see that everyone is really doing the best they can. Our bests are different, depending on experiences and circumstances, and I can't judge my best next to someone else's best.

Everybody *wants* to do it right. Sometimes one path is more challenging (and even harmful) than another path. And still, I believe everyone is doing the best that they can.

I remember not long after Travis died, my dear friend took me to Walmart. I had a broken leg. Going to Walmart was not a simple task. It was pouring down rain. I was in a wheelchair. It was a WHOLE situation.

After my friend got the wheelchair from the back of the car and brought it around to my side, I made my way from the passenger seat into the wheelchair, struggled to get the plank under my bum and thigh so my leg would be elevated, backed up in the wheelchair, grabbed my bags and closed the back of the car, all in the pouring rain.

As we finally headed in the direction of the entrance, the man who was parked next to us aggressively pulled out of his spot, slowed down to give us the stinkiest of stink eyes, and sped off. Apparently, we had taken too long getting ourselves situated, and he had to wait for us to leave before he could safely leave his spot.

I remember that I wanted to chase after him (in my wheelchair!) and let him know that just a week prior, my husband had died, and I had broken my leg, all in a 24-hour-period. I couldn't believe the nerve of that guy.

And even this guy, even he was doing the best that he could. While I wanted him to know my story so he could extend just a little bit of grace, maybe he had a story of his own.

If I approach people and situations with this understanding that *everyone* is doing the best they can, grace is the foundation.

When grace is the foundation, it is so much easier to focus on listening to understand, rather than to be understood.

When we start with grace, empathy becomes the natural response because we see pieces of ourselves, and our own journey, in others.

When we focus on grace, we become less concerned with being right and more concerned with learning along the way to getting it right.

And note to self: this love of grace is important to extend to others AND ourselves.

Let's focus on grace. And when we don't, let's focus on grace again.

KEEP SHARING

As I mentioned earlier, I really do try to make gratitude a daily practice. And I often shake my head as I consider all of the things that I am so grateful for. All. The. Things.

I am reminded of how truly privileged I am. There is a lot of struggle in this world right now. Many people are finding it extremely challenging to simply put food on the table.

And here I sit, making my list of all the things I am grateful for today.

This sets off a barrage of thoughts in this overthinking mind of mine.

- It is okay to want more, no matter where the starting point is
- I can be grateful and still struggle
- Gratitude does not only belong to the privileged
- What do I do with my privilege?

Gratitude and privilege. Hmmm. This is where I really start to pay attention. I don't want to feel guilt or shame for all that I am grateful for. Many of these things I was born with, and others I worked very hard to receive. I don't want to deny everything that brings me gratitude.

I also don't want to sit in my gratitude and revel in it all. I don't want to be grateful and stop there.

May my gratitude always *inspire* me to share.

May I always seek to be generous with all that I have.

May I always remain in a cycle of reflection, gratitude, share, and repeat.

Reflection: Stop and take the time to savour the moment. The good ones and the not-so-good ones.

Gratitude: Always come back to a place of gratitude. Be grateful for what I have and what I'm learning.

Share: Don't keep these insights to myself—share them in meaningful ways.

Repeat: On the daily!

Share my voice. Share my things. Share what I have learned. Share what I am struggling with. Share my love. Share my dreams.

As I build this future of mine, as I reach for my big dreams and goals, I want this mindset of sharing to be my guide. To plan for ways to share simultaneously with ways to prosper.

Reflection-Gratitude-Share-Repeat. Yes, please.

GETTING ON
WITH THINGS

Recently, I made the decision to take my wedding rings off. I cried every day for a week. For those of you who have ever lost your spouse, and you wore a wedding ring, I know you will agree, this is a big fucking deal. Rings are the symbol of your love and commitment. Taking them off is not done lightly. And I still don't know if I was ready to take them off. They still sit on my bathroom counter for me to see every day. For me, I knew that I wanted 'taking them off' to be about Travis and me. I didn't want to take them off in response to anything other than a knowing between us. And sitting in the sun on a September morning, I felt Trav nudge me, wanting me to know that he thought it was time.

So much of my grief journey has been about my incessant thoughts about getting on with things and what comes next.

From early on, I was borderline obsessed about this. I knew the time would come where healing would take place, but I was so deeply worried that this meant forgetting Travis. I also know myself. Love and connection are extremely important to me. It was possible, maybe even likely, that I may find love again. Although the idea of being in another relationship was the LAST thing I wanted, I thought about it a lot. And then I felt bad for thinking about it.

How would I ever be ready? Would I ever have sex again? If I did, how would I not cry the ENTIRE time? What about my wedding rings? When do I take them off? When is too soon or too long? How will I know?

I would lie in bed, my body *aching* for Travis, and wonder how in the world I would ever possibly love again. I just couldn't. And if I did, this man would have to be okay with me obsessively talking about Travis, and thinking about him, and wishing for him. (What? That would be normal, right? Most guys would be chill with this, right?)

It's just such a clear example of how healing is a *process*. We can't possibly imagine anything different than how we are currently feeling. And then we heal a little bit. And our feelings change a little bit. And we're a little bit less afraid.

It might seem like this is leading up to some story about meeting a new guy and finding love again. It's not. And I spend less time thinking about what comes next for me in the love department. I think perhaps this is because I've had my love story. I know what it's like to love deeply and all the struggles and joys that belong to that kind of love. So I don't feel a deep need to love again. I might—one day—and I might not. I'm okay with both.

WHAT ABOUT SEX?

I f I am to be honest, I actually have A LOT to say about this topic. And I've included and deleted it several times. In the spirit of vulnerability, I'm going deep (no pun intended!)

This is where my daughters, my parents, and people who are uncomfortable with me talking about sex should just casually skip to the next chapter.

Here's the deal. When your husband dies, his penis dies with him. And I know that sex isn't everything in a relationship, but it really is an important part when all of a sudden you don't have it anymore, and the prospects of having it any time soon are minimal. There are a million things that I miss about Travis that have nothing to do with sex. AND I REALLY MISS SEX!

When he first died (literally within days!), I went to my drawer of goodies and threw every toy and piece of lingerie into the trash—every single one. I'm still not sure why I did this. And why this was on my to-do list so soon after he died. I just couldn't possibly fathom any kind of sexual activity without him.

Confession: Travis is the only person I have ever had sex with. At the time we met, I believed it was important to save myself for marriage.

Also, at the time we met I had a really unhealthy understanding of my body. I thought I was fat (I was not), and I thought I was undesirable. I met Travis at a five-day retreat that focused on getting real with ourselves and self-growth. One of the activities we did, involved me getting dressed up as a cowgirl. No problem. Except that my group's understanding of a cowgirl involved wearing tight jeans. This was a STRETCH for me. I didn't feel comfortable in tight jeans because I thought I looked fat in tight jeans. I vividly remember walking into the lobby feeling so incredibly self-conscious. Travis was across the room. He walked directly to me and said, "Wow, you look great in those jeans!" I'm sure I blushed and brushed it off. But inside, that comment did a number on me. This was the first time I can remember that it was made perfectly clear that a guy was physically attracted to me—that I was desirable. That was the first of many firsts in the sex and sexuality department with Travis. Because of this, almost every thought, emotion, and action associated with sex belonged to Travis and Travis only. We had a healthy relationship of sharing and trusting each other with our bodies and openly exploring sexuality with each other. Okay, that might be a bit of a report card comment. The real deal: It was hard for me to allow myself to trust him with this aspect without feeling shame. And it was also hard for me not to judge him for his own experiences (that were FAR more advanced than my own). We did have a healthy relationship in this department, and we had to work hard to get there.

The idea of sharing any kind of sexual experience with anyone other than Travis was unimaginable to me.

So, time went on. A month. Maybe two. And I couldn't take it anymore. So, I took matters into my own hands—literally—and when finished, I sobbed uncontrollably. UNCONTROLLABLY. So I let that be for a while.

And time went on again. And then I couldn't take it anymore. And then I sobbed all over again.

I'm sure there's some science to the fact that every time I had an orgasm, it was a massive release of emotions and tears. But all I knew was that it left me undone.

And then, also in an odd way, it was one of the only ways that I felt connected to him. So it was a twisted mix of tears and connection. Talk about AND!

And time went on again. And then I couldn't take it anymore. And I didn't cry. And then I cried because I didn't cry. Lord, help me.

So, there's that. I miss sex.

And I also miss touch. Not just the leading up to sex kind of touch. The kind that just gently communicates that I am seen and loved. And the kind that allows me to communicate this same message to my love. Touching feet under the covers in bed. A tap on the bum in the kitchen. Running a hand through the other's hair. Bringing the other close in an embrace. A kiss hello. Touching the other's ear gently. Rubbing the other's shoulders at the end of a long day. Touching an arm as we walked by. These are the things I miss. It seems natural that I miss being on the receiving end of these little moments of love and affection. I do. I also miss loving someone in this way—showing my love through touch. One of the important pieces I remember my grief counsellor sharing with me was the significance of acknowledging that not only am I grieving all the love I received from Travis, I am also grieving all the love I *gave* to Travis.

Lying in bed alone at night is still hard sometimes. My poor dog gets A LOT of snuggles. I like to think this is getting easier. It probably is. And it also sends me into a shit storm of emotions when I consider that I could possibly fall in love again and share this with another human being.

SHOWING UP

I have a girlfriend who calls me every morning on my way to work. And she often calls me on the way home from work. These are never soul-baring conversations. They're a little check-in to see what's coming or how things are going. We often end these conversations abruptly, we interrupt each other all the time, and they're not very censored.

And they mean the absolute world to me.

I no longer have a person to kiss goodbye in the morning or to recap my day with in the evening. I don't have a person anymore who gets all the not-so-important details of my day. These daily phone calls make me feel connected in all the little ways that don't happen as often anymore.

And this is why girlfriends are deserving of big ass trophies with gold-plated humans holding a heart. Or a medal on a fat red, white, and blue ribbon that declares "Winner!"

Thank you, sweet Jesus, for girlfriends.

Because these women are just there.

When life falls apart, they are there.

When life is overflowing with joy, they are there.

When life is boring, and not much is worth reporting, they are there.

When I need encouragement, when I need a dance party, when I need a kick in the ass, when I need someone to believe in me until I can do that for myself, they are there.

When Trav died, they SHOWED UP.

And not just the first week, or month, or year. They continue to show up. And I know with my whole heart they will keep showing up. Some of these sisters I have known since childhood, some for less, and some are very recent sisters.

Moments after I found out about Trav, I was telling one of these gems on repeat, "My husband died, and I'm never going to see him again." And she gently guided me to a quiet, private spot and started making plans to get on a plane with me back home. There was no invitation, I didn't need to ask. It was a given that she was coming with me.

Then it was two weeks later, and I needed a lot of help due to my broken leg. Another one of these gems I speak of made the six-hour trip to come and stay with me. She left her own family of teenagers with all of their many, daily needs and she showed up.

And yet another one of these gems sat on the couch with me while I sobbed about the details of selling Trav's business and feeling overwhelmed and missing him with every single ounce of my being. She didn't say one single word. She just held my head on her chest, stroked my hair, and cried her own silent tears. She didn't ask me to stop; she didn't ask me to speak or explain; she just offered her unconditional love and presence.

These gems attended to every detail that went into planning a kick-ass celebration of life for Travis while I was on the couch nursing a broken leg. These gems love me, and listen to me, and feel for me. These gems cry their own real tears over my heartbreak. These gems send love notes in the mail, invite me to family barbeques, spend New Year's with me, listen to my worries, don't judge when I refer to Trav as SDH (stupid, dead husband), celebrate my success, and believe in me with their whole hearts.

Spouses are great. Parents are great. Children are great. Girlfriends are a special kind of something. They are not required or expected to show up. There is no piece of paper that legitimizes their commitment to us. They have made no vows. They show up because they *want to*. They extend these acts of love and generosity because they *choose to.*

These sisters have shown me what love looks like in action. They have inspired me to forever aim to be the kind of friend they have been to me. This journey of healing is cradled in their love.

LIVING YOUR LEGACY

S hit IS going to hit the fan. It isn't a question of if, but when. The question is, will you be ready for it?

I'm not talking about living a life in dreaded anticipation. I'm talking about living a life that is full of love, and empathy, and courage. Living a life that builds resilience.

How do you handle the small disappointments of life? Your friend cancelled your plans. The weather kept you from doing what you had hoped for. You didn't get the job you applied for. Your washing machine needs to be replaced, two weeks after you just replaced your dishwasher.

Building a life that cultivates character, love, respect, and hope not only creates our most beautiful life possible but also prepares us for when things get hard.

This human experience will break your heart. Guaranteed. And then there's also the little fact that our time will come when we leave this earth.

I know, Little Miss Cheerful over here.

My husband was not perfect. None of us are. He pissed some people off. And I can also say with 100 per cent confidence that he left this world with nothing left unsaid.

He did not have any unfinished business.

There is not one person who was important to him that didn't know how much they meant to him. He made things right when they went sideways.

He chased freedom with a vengeance and lived a life FULL of adventure.

He left this world the happiest he had ever been.

And that took a whole lot of work. He did the work. He had tough conversations. He looked deep into his heart. He regularly reflected on where he was and where he wanted to be.

What a gift.

Live THIS kind of life.

Live a life that is abundant with love and the things that fill your soul.

Live a life that prepares you for the day when your heart breaks, knowing there is a deep reserve within you that will get you through.

Live a life that cultivates relationships and builds a community of people around you who will pull you up when you need it.

Live a life you can be deeply proud of.

Don't wait. Do the work. It will see you through the darkness when it comes. And it will be your legacy when you leave.

FINDING BEAUTY
THROUGH THE
TATTERED

"While we grieve, and feel, and lament, and express
whatever it is that is brewing within us, a truth courses
through our veins of all our bumps and bruises, and it is
this: We have received. You're here. You're breathing. And
you received a gift. A generous, extraordinary, mysterious,
inexplicable gift. "
-Rob Bell, *Everything is Spiritual*

I n our current home, Trav put a flagpole in our backyard
and hung a pirate flag on it. Yes, the skull and crossbones
one that you're thinking of is the one. And it proudly waved
above the tiki bar he also built in our backyard. On several
occasions, he would ring the bell, letting me know it was
Happy Hour, don me with a Hawaiian lei, and pass me a pina
colada while Jimmy Buffet played in the backyard. I'm not
making this up.

Two months after Trav died, on a beautiful January morning,
I sat staring out my window at this flag. I remember noticing
the contrast between the flag, which was now tattered by the
wind, and the sun peaking over the mountains in the distance.
Clouds were making their way across the sky, covering and
uncovering the light from the sun. I couldn't help but see the
metaphor. In the forefront was tattered me—ripped apart by
the loss of Travis. I was all over the place, with reminders of
him imprinted all over me. But behind that, in the distance, I

saw beauty. The sun was shining on the mountains and water. The wind would rise up, giving the flag what it needed to fly. And then the wind would die down and the flag would lie still. Trav was the wind that was giving me what I needed to fly. Then the wind would go away and leave me flattened. I remember focusing on that flag, *feeling* that flag. And there was also a small part of me that was acknowledging the beauty behind it. Knowing it was there. Knowing there would be a time when I could focus on the beauty and when I would *feel* the beauty. And trusting that this time would come.

I read the quote at the start of this chapter on the very last day of my Sip, Love, Safari trip. And it seemed to summarize so much of my learning and healing from that trip. I scribbled some thoughts to Trav in my journal...

Your life is such a gift to me. What a gift to be your wife— your partner. To live life with you and to parent our beautiful daughters together, to struggle together. And then find such joy, happiness, and contentment together.

Being without you in this world is not a gift. And yet, perhaps the life and opportunities that it has and will bring me is. Perhaps loving you and being loved by you in this new way is a gift.

I've struggled with this concept so hard! I feel like I shouldn't even use the word *gift* in the same context as Trav dying. So, let me be clear: Trav's dying will NEVER be a gift. Never, ever in a million years.

His life was an absolute gift.

The lessons I have learned since his death are a gift.

The growth within myself is a gift.

The opportunity to have conversations about grief with others is a gift.

The creativity and generosity that has blossomed since his death is a gift.

Writing this book, and sharing my journey with you, is such a gift.

I've been learning a lot about grief and its connection to creativity, to creating something new. Rob Bell gives a beautiful image in his book, *Everything is Spiritual*. He's talking about the very first image in the Bible in the book of Genesis. Where everything is undefined, no form, and darkness is over the water. He explains that the water symbolizes the unknown, the abyss. And then,

"Spirit enters into those waters and out of them creates something new. Something vast and expansive and beautiful and diverse."

It has taken me a while to allow this to sink into my heart. I have heard versions of this often. And I haven't really been ready to hear them. I didn't want something new. I wanted what I already had with Travis. Perhaps as the reality of his being gone sets deep into my bones, this message will more easily penetrate my heart.

I am beginning to see this beautiful new creation. Looking back in my journal, I see that I have always known it was there.

Since Trav died, sunrises have become a daily reminder of this beauty in my life. They made an appearance on the morning after he died, delighted me on my Sip, Love, Safari trip, and I am so grateful to wake up to their beautiful greeting many mornings from my bedroom window.

They continue to remind me that each day is a new start, a new gift. While I continue to miss Travis on so many levels, I can also say that I am excited to see what the future will bring. That's been a struggle and is hard to even say. I don't for a second want to give the impression that I am excited to live this life without my husband. I am not. A million times over, I would choose to have my husband back here with me. To hear his voice and his laugh, feel his touch and his scruffy face, and to do all the life things together—all of them—oh, Sweet Jesus.

This life is no longer available to me. And I will not let the death of Travis define me. It is not the end of my story. It is a critical part of my story. And it's not the whole thing.

What I am excited about is continuing to discover new ways to live this life to the fullest, in honour of Travis AND in honour of myself. To create something new and so beautiful that it softens the edges of my broken heart and ignites in me a passion for creating a life I never dreamed possible. And to do so with Travis cheering me on, proud of this new version of myself, and being a part of this next great adventure in ways we never imagined.

Eventually, I took that pirate flag down. The tattered reminder is no longer there. The clouds still are, from time to time. It's still not always easy to see the beauty. The clouds will always roll in and out—that's life. My focus is the beauty now. Seeing it and chasing it with everything I have.

ALWAYS, AND

I have a tattoo on my right hip. I got it a year after Travis died. It's a sketch of a mountain with words "Always, and" written in his handwriting underneath it. It's a daily reminder.

Always, and.

I will ALWAYS miss Travis, AND I can live a life with joy and meaning. I can pursue new things, I can create new dreams, and I can have moments or even a full day that isn't consumed with memories of him.

I will ALWAYS feel this hole in my heart that only he can fill. Trav was one of a kind and will always have a part of me. AND living this life to the very fullest helps heal this heart. Planning new adventures, learning new things, and finding joy in the moment is the medicine that helps me move forward.

I will ALWAYS love Travis, AND there are so many amazing and loving people in my life that I am incredibly grateful for.

Giving and receiving love with Trav is not really an option anymore. But giving and receiving love from all of the people in my life has become so much more meaningful. There is A LOT of love in the hearts of humans (and my sweet Bernie dog). Soaking up this love, and giving it freely and generously, fills my heart.

It's a thing, moving forward from the death of someone you loved. A hard thing. And it happens whether you want it to or not. You move forward. And then you move back a little. And then you move forward again. I know this is the process. I know it's healthy to move forward. And most days I feel okay about it.

And some days it still breaks my heart. Moving forward still feels like moving away. I don't want the distance.

I will ALWAYS feel this heartache, AND I am okay.

I share this journey in hopes of better understanding my own process and also helping others feel a bit more seen or understood with their own journey. In doing so, I am healing. Sharing the hard parts helps me be more okay. And my hope is that on some level, it helps you be more okay, too. I am healing, I am learning, I am growing, and I am okay.

Always, and...

Made in the USA
Coppell, TX
29 July 2021

59669851R00056